GW00792339

FROM *Moon Light* TO STREET LIGHT

and The Thief

DEANE P O'DONNELL

authorHOUSE®

(handwritten signature)
2025

*enjoy
from
Deanne*

AuthorHouse™ UK
1663 Liberty Drive
Bloomington, IN 47403 USA
www.authorhouse.co.uk
Phone: UK TFN: 0800 0148641 (Toll Free inside the UK)
UK Local: (02) 0369 56322 (+44 20 3695 6322 from outside the UK)

Published by AuthorHouse 03/06/2025

ISBN: 979-8-8230-9222-7 (sc)
ISBN: 979-8-8230-9224-1 (hc)
ISBN: 979-8-8230-9223-4 (e)

Library of Congress Control Number: 2025904703

Print information available on the last page.

CONTENTS

Introduction vii

Chapter 1: The Bogside Riot 1

Chapter 2: From Moon Light 5

Chapter 3: Yehoshua..9

Chapter 4: Joe's Coffee shop 13

Chapter 5: To Streetlight.. 19

Chapter 6: The Interview... 25

Chapter 7: Family gossip 31

Chapter 8: And the Thief 35

Acknowledgement of Charity 41

INTRODUCTION

The stories, in this book are the testimony of events that have happened with the Divine supernatural showing, Real light, To The birth child Son Yehoshua of Our Lady. The Holy Immaculate Conception. You the reader, Have total reassurance to know the ruling powers of this world "Have proven the Absolute Supreme Divine Authority of the Messiah Yehoshua -Jesus" With no confusion of the mind or any Deception to your own soul You Have the guarantee, for Yehoshua the Messiah "Did show, Heaven's military supremacy" of our one Divine Holy God to Earthly children and the Divine Holy Angels that God provides to us "For Free" as is our God in the details of living life.

Chapter One
THE BOGSIDE RIOT

*W*ITH MORE THAN EIGHT HUNDRED years of war and millions of Christian people terrorised as they journey A living life on the island of Ireland. The two Christian faiths "The Roman Catholics and the English Protestants.

On one summer's day, in the late nineteen nineties, Patrick and some of his friends were playing football along the river bank. suddenly a school friend Stevie, Came Running over to them saying "British soldiers are in the Bogside. Will? we go down to have a look? there is rioting going on" saying again "will we go?" asking them all. As young teenagers they were all excited and agreed "yes" and run over to the Bogside to have a look at the Rioting with the British army. "the Brits" were firing live rubber bullets at the protestors, when they arrived at the riot. the sky was dark and everyone was ecstatic At seeing the large crowd rioting and noticing cars and vans were burning on fire in the middle of the roads "A real riot" as Patrick had seen on television news. seeing mostly older people, With about a hundred people throwing stones and petrol bombs towards the soldiers and the armoured vehicles from behind a barricade. People were refuelling others with bins full of beer bottles, some wearing balaclavas. Patrick and his friends started to pick up stones from the ground and throwing them towards the English army. After ten minutes or so? A person walked over to Patrick and his friends, he was wearing a balaclava then saying, to then in a loud voice. "go home now, this is not the place for You's. You are too young to be here, go home now, go home immediately" as he pointed in the opposite direction. So they immediately dropped the stones to the ground and quickly moving away from the corner of the wall they we're standing at, watching. Patrick seen a petrol bomb, hitting the roof of Jacky Mullins bar. Setting the building's roof on fire. suddenly, Patrick felt something hit, his Left foot. on looking down to seeing and realising a rubber bullet just reflected off his foot. Shocking Patrick At that moment one of the other spectators, went running over and picking up the rubber bullet from the ground. then asking Patrick "is it ok. to keep it, I've been trying all night, to get one" "yes" Patrick replied. Arron called out, "It's too dangerous for us to be here, let's go" So the four of them left the Bogside and went back to the community park. still Excited and talked about what happened, that evening. Everyone got home safely to their family's and love ones. thanks to God.

The next day, On the local television news revealed, "that a person was killed, the night before at a riot in the Bogside area of Londonderry" this was the first and last riot, Patrick and his friends were at. "As time is God" over twenty years later? Patrick was standing in the stairway of a building with others, between takes. One, of the other new work mates for the day. said to Patrick "Jacky Mullins bar you were there at that riot? he was there also that time. But On the other side. do you remember the riot" asking? Patrick replied. "yes, that's right, That was over twenty-five years ago? and he was not there, that time "when the IRA, told him and his friends to go home, "immediately" they were too young to be there and not to be throwing stones at You's. You are right, you have me mixed up with someone else, as You's were not In Amsterdam in the year of the Lord, twenty twelve" it was all pictures and no sound" for the rest of the day.

Chapter Two
FROM MOON LIGHT

THE SUN AS RAISED TO us a new day now with the coronavirus nineteen "Pandemic emergency" active in forced from city to cities around the world "the Global lockdown. for everyone" Patrick was desperate to find somewhere to stay? Finally finding a hostel open with booking.

The hostel had people staying from all sides of the world Argentina, Brazil, China, England, Germany, Holland, Ireland, Portugal and Spain. Bill from New Zealand with his "war stories" and Ben from England with the company car (a new Tesla electric) a few weeks later, in to the lockdown.

Patrick was stepping up from the beach at the back of the hostel. the two undercover spies. Bill & Ben are talking to each other at the garden table. Patrick overhearing them "Bill says to Ben We will say. "he attacked you" Ben is standing and immediately reached down and picked up a knife, from the green garden table and placing it behind his left arm, Ben is 6'4 and army trained. Patrick was now standing at the opposite end of the garden table ready to battle. At that moment, Zen the French journalist "walked out from the building and down the steps, then stood on the other side of the garden" Ben seen, Zen and immediately placed the knife back on to the table in front of them. Ben "Shrugging his shoulders, and saying to Patrick "it is what it is. You know that" Patrick replied. "your right, It is what it is" And "released his hand from the side of the plastic garden table" he was going to use for protection from attack. "Zen was keeping open eyes and ears on everyone. As she keep looking towards to the water at the paradise view" Ben then asked? Patrick with a serious manner in his voice "Have you ever seen the moon up close? Like really up close? with the giant crater holes and all, Have you?" Patrick replied. "yes, I've seen the moon up close and so have others? The moon apparition in Donegal, was a Divine message for the peacekeepers and for others. You know? that our Lord is true and You's cannot win any war or defeat Yehoshua in anyway? A word of advice? About that moonlight Apparition from the Messiah" (At) three government officers witnessed the Apparition and the massive size of the moon to the Earth and Our human size with God. Patrick said. "for us living on the earth at this time. this will happen in the future and the Lord will provide us with protection from it" then God. Showed them. A Very clear visible shining light On to the road they were traveling. (From the moonlight) Our lord and Saviour, our Divine protection of the soul from the bite of evil. (God. Demonstrated a very safe road to Follow, for them physically and with faith in the truth to the person Yehoshua -Jesus. Patrick said "he is the guarantee and he is our guarantor for your soul's our security from the bite of evil. "Understand

God will always answer your prayers, one way or another? In the beginning of life, in the middle of life, and at the end of life".

Yehoshua will always be there for us and to lead us with his Divine protection, for all souls of good Dignity towards Heaven.

Chapter Three
YEHOSHUA

*I*T's A COLD AND WET day in the workplace with some Hollywood super star actors, We're on set with undercover security and spies all over the place. Patrick was informed by his line manager "do not speak to any of the actors on less they talk to you first" Patrick did not speak to any of them Patrick had no reason to anyway Patrick's New work mate, Mr Fox said, to Patrick one day "he was at a riot in the Bogside. Over twenty years ago. you were at it, let's say you got one of my rubber bullets that day, am not just the cook you know" "they both laughed" then Mr Fox said. to

Patrick "my lord Jesus Christ, has me working with you now, as we provide security for others" then saying, "Can I say? the above management and leadership knows Jesus, has risen and the Lord has showed us, true kindness from God. to our souls with the Lord's forgiveness for our sins as we have also been deceived by others, we English people also prey to our lord for help and to help our family's, we are all born on this earth into a family and country, it is how God has it. we have all been wronged and did wrong by the "lies" of others, we believe in our faith and the truth of the man. Jesus the son of God and the virgin Mary. yes, we know who she is" (Yehoshua, Our one Divine Holy God. Now and forever the person that has shown to all of us the faithful and the condemned the safest path to follow for our personal soul. with the sun and the moon every day providing us with light As God has proven for us, Providing the words and actions of truth to the person, the Messiah. the true light and forever as guaranteed by himself (Yehoshua) the birth child of the (Holy Immaculate Conception our lady Mary) with full

Authority of our one Divine Holy God. our lord we pray and

to God we pray thankfully every day and every night with

hundreds and millions and billions of other people living

that all pray to God, for their own reasons without judgment

or embarrassment or shame to God)

Chapter Four
JOE'S COFFEE SHOP

PING SOUNDS FROM THE MOBILE phone all morning It's an advert, become a member of our community coffee club you must age 18 + years old, So Patrick pinpointed the location and started a Google Maps Adventure In Barcelona. in a big city by Now well outside his understanding of the street's locations or what doors to nock and not fully understanding the language excited with the adventure experience. In the hot Mediterranean weather. a few hours later with all the travel from bus to tram to walking and seeing thousands of new people with beautiful Hermosa buildings (Sagrada Basilica) Patrick finely making it to Joe's coffee shop with passport for identity. The cafe shop in size was small holding about twenty people comfortable. three people were leaving and they offer the corner table to Patrick (Now in a trap) Patrick said. "Thanks" to them as they pass by him. Them also living a life on earth on a Holy journeys to God. Patrick got comfortable testing the cannabis seed. With music for the soul playing in the back ground. Patrick was minding his own business and then noticed six young lads speaking, English. on looking passed them at the television on the wall behind them, Mr sunglasses said, to the others, "He's here now and nodding towards Patrick and saying, "they will be here shortly" then looking at his Mobile phone. Patrick thought that was very odd. Then One of the others then said, "Where Definitely getting something to eat on the way back am starving" another replied. "That's for sure, am totally stoned" they all United in happiness and started to laugh out loud. Patrick did not recognize them Or knew of any meeting with them,

So giving it no more thought. About ten minutes later, Patrick gets dry mouth and visits next door to get a soft lemonade drink as the cannabis coffee shop did not sell soft drinks. agreement with city council and other independent retail business. On Returning back in from the shop next door to the social club. On entering and seeing the place was empty? on walking to his table. The host, behind the counter give Patrick "A what the fuck look" and walks in to the side office and closed the door. a man and woman was seating at the table next to his. The place had only three people and Patrick, Now at the table beside them, in the corner of the room with only one way in and one way out. That could only be used. Patrick was looking at the television, it was showing. La Sagrada Families basilica" On looking over at the table, the people had nothing in front of them not even a cuppa? Patrick knew then something was definitely up? Patrick softly Heard their thoughts and said, to them out a Loud "in just you're wondering? to any questions of the reasons Why? He did not know why?

Yehoshua asked him to show a message from Heaven that You's have answered true. The set up in Amsterdam, yes Jesus has risen and You's can prove it. The soul of a man and the soul of a woman from water to dust to flesh and our soul to God" The woman. looked at Patrick with a disbelief and confused look? the man, he was smiling from ear to ear as if he had won the euro millions jack pot (For he knew (the set-up) did happen) A true believer in Jesus with other private words said. Reassuring the soldiers of Yehoshua from other men that my say they are him? with a real event that happed a few months before. Patrick said "do you remember? a House party that he was at in Malaga. You have helped them human souls that you have never meet before? You have helped all them people, to a safer and better life. They have prayed to yehoshua Jesus and his mother Mary, and that's a fact. If you what to go there? for their own reasons, I think you know the reasons why? and by the way "Thank you For helping them people"

Patrick finished his coffee and Left the social club making his way to get the munchies. (Something to eat)

"Be guaranteed the Divine truth of Yehoshua is working his love of charity and peace every day for our protection for his family"

Chapter Five
TO STREETLIGHT

LATE ONE EVENING, PATRICK IS walking home peacefully minding his own business just looking to go to sleep, It was a long week at work, moving business and busses from one country to another. Suddenly, Patrick heard a soft voice from above him Saying, Hello. On looking up Patrick could see, three massive Divine Angels that were glowing in gold. wearing monk robes with no face just a soft voice and the total darkness behind them, they were looking down over all of us on earth Having "The absolute Authority of the living God. Then Patrick noticing in the far-off distance, appeared the parents of friends that had died years before. They Were On a path walking side by side holding hands with luggage. Patrick thought that was very odd? As the massive Gate of Heaven was Open for all the souls on the path to words the Holy Sanctuary of Heaven. Patrick seeing up as one piece of sand and the Absolute size of God. then one of the Angels. asked, Patrick do you see that, As they pointed at the street light and underneath was a gold sports car. It was all rusted and neglected with flat tires and blocking the front gate and public foot path of a single mothers Home, Patrick was thinking, it was one of the family member that lives there? Patrick said. "what's it got to do with him, it does not belong to him or his family" on looking closer to the parents. they looked over to Patrick and the mother called out the name of their youngest child. "Keith" and telling Patrick "he paid, for it with money from drugs, the bad ones his father was at the meeting about. We think you should know" then Keith's father called over to him. Saying "he told me you called in that day" (he was at a meeting About Keith) and he was praying to our lord and Saviour yehoshua Jesus and Saint padre pio. for his youngest child's safety)

"We ask your help" His mother said. Patrick noticing again the luggage bag's they were holding. Patrick was confused? then Immediately remembered. The appearance of Yehoshua to him in the back garden of their family home that time. (Giving Patrick a message for Keith)

"To Stop his anti-social crimes and the supply of a dangerous drug to teenagers"

(Keith had already got an appointment time for that evening to be kneecapped by shooting (by a named group) Patrick was Powerless to do anything to stop it. As he did not know nothing about the issue? Or about the previous warnings told to Keith To stop)

(That day. Patrick got up from the kitchen table to go and on turning round and looking out the kitchen window. Suddenly. appeared Yehoshua in a sandy gold robe with white strings around his waist with hands together. telling

Patrick the message for Keith "tell him, the Lord has heard your fathers Prayer's and yours to" no act of violence will happen" but you must stop, the path you are on" Keith was seating at the kitchen table and remarks the brightness in the room around Patrick at that time.)

Then Another Angel appeared from behind the three saying to Patrick "it's not his? its other people's and he is being used. he intends to leave it there for years and to forget about it. putting their rubbish in the front of other people's home and they live miles away. A child will be knocked down also you will hear" Then pointed down towards the street light, Immediately a silver and white light shoots from its hand as they pointed and saying, "there you go, that's what you do with rubbish" surprised and stepping back at seeing the gold car was on fire. then Patrick seeing the two parent's souls they grow up tall and the large luggage bags disappeared that they We're holding and seeing them disappear as a white light in to the Open gate and hearing the singing of Holy prayers.

As Patrick was looking around to the path and Seeing on the path was millions of other souls on their Holy journey to heaven gate, they were receiving Divine Blessing from God with protection from their Angel's helping out and also seeing souls falling off the side of the road. not knowing why? Patrick asked. the Angel "why is that" the Angel replied. "they have chosen their own path and rejected God. For ever soul in every generation is all knowing by god personally the individual soul of each? They all once lived a life on earth at one time and knew of god. They all prayed to the Lord for help. most of them in true faith to God and we did provide Blessings to their soul, But for them others You see falling? they only prayed to the Lord, to try and deceive God".

Chapter Six
THE INTERVIEW

*I*T'S ANOTHER RAINY DAY WITH the sun shining through the dark clouds, the rain started to fall heavier, Patrick decided to drop in to a pub he was just passing In town after ordering a drink Then Seating at the bar counter looking out at the rain suddenly, a man seats, beside Patrick, asking Patrick "would he be ok to meet with some of his friends, they would like to answer some of your questions, that you might have. a wee chat like, we think you know what it's about" Patrick replied, "yes" and thought, he did know, Why and there is no way he was going to out run them people. Then the person poured white powder into Patricks drink. Saying "you are going to need this it will help and smiled would you meet us at naming the place in ten minutes" then patting Patrick on the shoulder as he left. Patrick finished his drink then walked up the hill to meet the people He did not know? The heavy rain had stopped now. At the other pub, On entering the Barmaid went on the phone saying, "that fella, you're looking for is here now" as she Looked over at him. Patrick told the woman the reason for the men looking to talk with him, her face changed to disbelief and a confused look. a few moments later three men walked in. Helping Patrick up from his seat and asking was he "ok" as the white powder was definitely kicking in, taking affect. when getting into the waiting car. Patrick Seen another car with company logos on it at the corner blocking the road. Then one of the interviewers poked Patrick in the eyes, a few minutes later on entering to a house, Patrick opened his eyes on hearing a child's voice saying "mum who's that man?" the mother replying, "he is a friend of Daddies, they want to talk with him just, let's go in here and put the cartoons on" "Yes" the child said. As the child waved over to him. Patrick Replying, with a friendly reassurance smile. Then walking up the stairs into a room for his first part of the interview? Seating on a chair and then they tied his legs and hands to the side of the chair. Tim asking again "who? do you work for Just Tell us, every body works for somebody. This will go easier for you, Just tell us who you work for? we will find out" seating up on the seat looking all around him, it was dark with just a dim light from the other room. Patrick said. to them "Yehoshua the man you call Jesus that person you prey to every day for help or if you don't it's none of my business. Him who has risen from death with the Divine Authority of God. The Messiah Yehoshua that's his real name. He is my boss go see him, just so you know it's all good Well maybe not for everyone?" Tim said. to Patrick "You are a Lier. How dear you bring the Lord's name in to it, it's ok to tell us we can keep a secret. Because if you think you're so smart, we have people shitting in your toilet and there is fuck all you can do about it, so make me a cuppa tea, you're a cunt" Tim then kneeled down closer with a dislike look and placing his hand on Patrick's leg and saying he has killed others" Patrick replied. "well guess, who is waiting on you in the afterlife" Another person was standing behind Patrick and their Mobile phone buzzed, then he said to the others "quickly fry his head up again before he comes around anymore, We're leaving" Two, of the other interviewers started shouting loudly into Patrick's ear's causing him blinking out again, A moment later walking down the stairs to leave, the woman was at the Living room door all smiles. Patrick, said. "thanks to the woman for his visit to her home" noticing one of the interviews face with the shock look of surprise at the seriousness of event with people outside in cars. They quickly all moved over to the Military base to visit doctors for a more physical and psychological interview (a wee chat) With hypnoses and deep brain washing on the menu when Patrick was finished his interview. waiting in a dark room, one of the interviewers said to Patrick this was nothing personal On him, they do this as part of the Job, It's a thing they do. at that moment. as other person walked in to the room, telling the others saying, "you're never going to believe how they are bringing in now. then asking something to them. one replied, ok. Then the person and another helping Patrick up and asking Patrick was he "ok" " yes, am ok, thanks for asking" Patrick replied. as they both burst out laughing. Then Patrick blinked out with exhaustion from the interview. Patrick was not the first person to have this interview done for sure a profound mind brain washing experiencing and seeing in others many years later with old school friends and other two face people. Patrick remembered his own interview with the ruling powers of an army. (Yehoshua is a real person with the Divine knowledge of God. For our soul's path? that show the reasons Why the Lord's ways work the best. Yehoshua the Messiah. He Has walked on the earth Before us and will walk on earth after us and has showed us the path to follow to Gods Holy Sanctuary of Heaven, that truly is a real place for us all. "Only the evil sinner keeps themselves out of Heaven".

Chapter Seven
FAMILY GOSSIP

*I*T'S ANOTHER BEAUTIFUL DAY IN the north of Ireland, the sun is shining between the heavy rain showers, Patrick went to visit his parents, mid-day, walking to the Corner shop for milk and biscuits, on passing a neighbour's Home "Keith was standing at the front door and called Patrick in to visit for a few minutes" Patrick was preparing a family meal later that day in the kitchen and heard the front door opening and a Loud voice calling out, "hello. it's only me, are you in" recognising the voice. as his mother's Lifelong friend. His mother replied, "yes, am in" As she walked in to the living room. Saying, "you're never going to believe what happened" that's the normal conversation opening, (drama) As the visitor noticed Patrick "she give him a dirty look" then saying to Patrick in an angry voice. "go and put the kettle on and make us a cuppa tea, go on. Now" Patrick thought of her, not nice words at all. Patrick replied. "sure, I'll put the kettle on but you make your own tea and my mother a cup, you're not here to visit me, are you?" the visitor she giving Patrick another dirty look. Patrick left the living room, as he did not care, for her drama. About an hour later, Patrick was in the kitchen again and his father arrived home from work early to the visiting in-law. Patrick said, to his Father jokingly, what bring ye home at this time. As it's was a few hours earlier than normal. His father replied, "Nothing to do down there. Standing about, all of the machines are out on-site work, going for a wee sleep now, am getting old am in my sevenths now you know?" Suddenly, in a loud aggressive voice, the visitor said. to Patrick and his father, do not interrupt us when we're talking" then saying. to Patrick's Father "make us a cuppa tea, Do something useful with yourself, As she give him a dirty look and pointing at the kitchen. Patrick and his father was taking back at the rudeness and disrespect, she has showed to them one to many times. Patrick knew then. "she was the family spy Tim talked of" Patrick said. to the visitor "he was not making her tea ever again, for sure you have had over fifty cups" the visitor laughed knowingly. She has totally taken advantage of the family kindness and family friendship for many a long years, they visit a lot, so they can get private information to pass on to others. covered over by sugar and salt "you can tell me, were family" With no real blame to them for also being hypnotised and having been interviewed by the army's intelligence branch and With one other feck best friend to his mother. would reveal the reason for their visit of friendship. They did bring one night stands back from the pub, to sleep with in her friend's home, as they sleep safely in their private home. there is still hope in God's forgiveness for the sins of another that have been deceived, also on their Holy Divine journey to God, for the soul, May the lord show us education in his many reasons of living life in the heart and mind and soul to God. Yehoshua Has risen. Yehoshua has spoken. Yehoshua has shown and yehoshua has proven for us all. How believe to ask for his help in morals and Prey's with action for good .

Chapter Eight
AND THE THIEF

*I*T'S ANOTHER, BEAUTIFUL HOT DAY on the Paradise island, at ten forty-five, in the morning, it's, twenty-eight, Celsius. Patrick with one of his new work mates, were walking down town, a Hermosa Paradise world. then Paul asked. Patrick, "was he? In the IRA. like his friends are? you can tell me, I can keep a secret" Patrick replied. "No, You could be in the IRA For all I know And for my so-called friends? Pat, we have never meet before" Paul said. "You have and Pat is telling the team Your lifelong buddies" Patrick Replied. "I do not know him. Yes, John is an old school friend. But we have not spoken for more than twenty years. because John was and still is a dangerous back stabbing liar. John is Sick in the head. A condemned soul Starting trouble and causing problems with everyone in the work place. No friend to me at all. We would be standing beside John at different times, "as you know Paul" having to listening to how great he is. You heard that yourself the other evening! we both Heard? What one of the Spanish women said to him. "(Eres una persona enferma y repugnante, Esperamos que mueras de una muerte horrible, demonio)" As they smiled at him when they said it. And John thought? they were saying. nice words about him. (Paul laughs, knowing John's behaviour was totally disrespectful to the Spanish and to the Irish people)

(This become very obvious by the thieves over the working weeks)

Patrick was embarrassed to be from the same city. Patrick said. to Paul "The Lord, he reminds us, we have a personal free will to self-direct our life and our soul, for yehoshua will reject people and their calls for help" Paul then started patting his chest with his fist and said to Patrick "he was in "MI" and we know all about you to Holy man" Paul was trying on a pair of sunglasses then asked. Patrick "do these suit me?" Patrick replied. "am surprised that you can get a pair to fit you with that size of head" sarcastically, Paul replied. "You cheeky fucker, don't you worry, I don't Care what you think? They suit me" then going to the till and buying them. Suddenly. Patrick remembered Paul from many years before. As part of the interview with mi. The weeks they turned into years working the nightshift. eating, sleeping, traveling, watching, checking keys and locks. Repeat day in, day out. providing military security for all the Staff and visitors to the island. As is our own time visiting the island of Earth under God. (Yehoshua is the true light for our souls with his compassion and empathy to the forgiveness of sins, in this life and providing us with the divine protection from the dark bite of evil. Your Divine security for the soul)

After finishing his work, Patrick decided to Go on a Holy Pilgrimage To Fatima in Portugal for a few days after working the night shift for months. time to Switch off from work mode. One day Patrick was walking around town sightseeing and praying in the Holy sanctuary of Fatima. The heat was in the high twenties. too hot for Patrick, so he stepped in to a cafe bar to get some shade from the sun. ordering a drink and relaxing at a table in the side-garden with beautiful weather on a visit to Portugal. A few minutes later? Patrick heard a soft voice say. Hi you make the call to Paul now. Patrick was surprised and On looking up to the sky were the sound came from. He immediately seen a massive Divine Angel. In a gold robe just looking at him. Patrick replied. "no, I wants nothing to do with them, he was at the interview you know that" "no" Patrick said again "and for them other two What the fuck like? What have you got me in to? They are two total dick heads, You heard what the Spanish were saying to them and about them" The Angel said. in a louder voice "call that person now" as they pointed to the Mobile phone in front of him. "call him now" Saying again. Patrick said. "Ok, ok. I'll call him, I don't see the point?" (but Patrick has learned the hard way over the years by not listening to the Divine Angels when they speak from God) "You will know the reason for the theft?" then said. so Patrick makes the call. By texting a message to Paul About the other line manager on the (security job) "with the story of theft by the other line Manager "As time is God, in under one minute the thief called Patrick upset, saying, "why did you tell him? I stool from you" Patrick replied "because you did, over a thousand pounds my friend or are we meant to be comrades Here" The Thief ended the call immediately. Still having the stolen money. Patrick "knew" that the money was gone and spent already on his new sports jeep and also knew the line manager had been interviewed also with MI. Patrick Looked up to the Angel and the Angel said. to Patrick "by No fault of his own. a few times doing, you see the job they have him do and he has children also. As for your other friend, jokingly said. well he has chosen his own path and he thinks he's the man" Patrick suddenly remembers the screams from Hell "at his meeting with Yehoshua in Lourdes" you are meant to help us. fuck you anyway they said. to the Lord and now they all called out to God. in loud sorrowful cries. "Pleading and asking god to Forgive them" for their evil sins towards others as their souls lived and travelled a living life on earth. the Angel then disappeared and in under ten seconds. the man-made Mobile phone battery died and shutting down with a beep.

This showed to Patrick all is knowing to God. The real supernatural Divine Authority of intelligence by the Angels of god. for us all, towards understanding the truth in Yehoshua our salvation to Heaven's kingdom. now and forever with love to God.

ACKNOWLEDGEMENT OF CHARITY

Wishing to thank all the people with many Blessings that have made the stories of testimony possible with their own actions and life on earth, their own Holy journey. In the lords Truth. Our Lord is Providing the Divine Authority with charity guidance to help families and friends behind the scenes of social media, when needed, the people's kindness to others with empathy to the truth of other people living. the morals they hold and the respect they show with the trust in Yehoshua and our Lady and God. For all faith of religion guide Us all to God. providing charity of love to the families. on our own Holy journey to God, to enjoy with are living God, Yehoshua, is the Messiah. of Divine Truth and Light by the one god for us all to Prey know and follow if needing help to the real place of the Divine Heaven. All is welcome in.

God, Bless you.

www.ingramcontent.com/pod-product-compliance
Ingram Content Group UK Ltd.
Pitfield, Milton Keynes, MK11 3LW, UK
UKHW040626230325
456598UK00001B/6